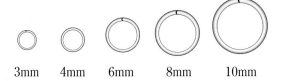

3mm 4mm 6mm 8mm 10mm

Jump Rings

Premade jump rings are avail[...]
opened and closed using Chain n[...]

Popular sizes are available in gold and silver-plated finishes.

To make jewelry fast and easy, most of the projects in this book were made with premade jump rings.

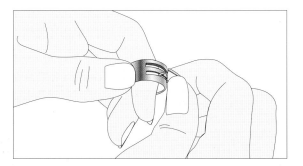

Jump Ring Tool

Wear the tool on your finger and use it to open and close jump rings with ease. Simply insert a jump ring in one of the three slots and twist to open or close.

Use the tool in combination with Chain nose pliers, or use two tools at a time.

How to Make Your Own Jump Rings

Make the jump rings you need - in the size and wire gauge you want.

The *Beadalon* Jump Ring Maker comes in 8 round sizes (16, 14, 12, 10, 8, 7, 6 and 4mm) of metal mandrels to create your own round or oval jump rings. Thick coiled wires add definition and texture to jewelry designs. Handmade jump rings in a thick gauge wire were used for the Byzantine Chain bracelet on page 16.

Use gold-filled, sterling silver, colored or base metal wire to fashion components that complement your jewelry designs.

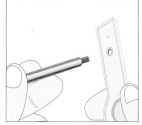   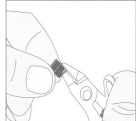 

Step 1. Choose a mandrel based on the desired jump ring size. Screw the mandrel into the base.

Step 2. Insert wire into the small hole in the base. Fold wire down to secure it.

Step 3. Insert your finger into the large hole in the base and turn clockwise while holding the mandrel and wire in the other hand.

Step 4. Once the wire is coiled, remove it from the base and cut with a Flush Cutter tool.

Step 5. Now you can make the right-size jump rings in the colors you choose any time!

How to Make Twisted Jump Rings

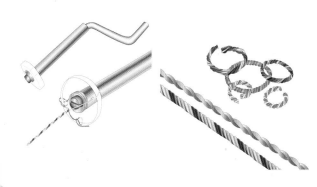

Use a Wire Twister to make twisted jump rings for jewelry. It is easy to use, fast and fun. Place up to 5 wires onto the disc of the twister, then attach these wires to a sturdy object. Pull the wires taut, turn the crank and watch the wires twist. Use color and size combinations to create great looking rings.

Once twisted, use the Jump Ring Maker to create different sizes of round or oval jump rings. Tip. Multiple wires, once twisted, have more strength than single wires.

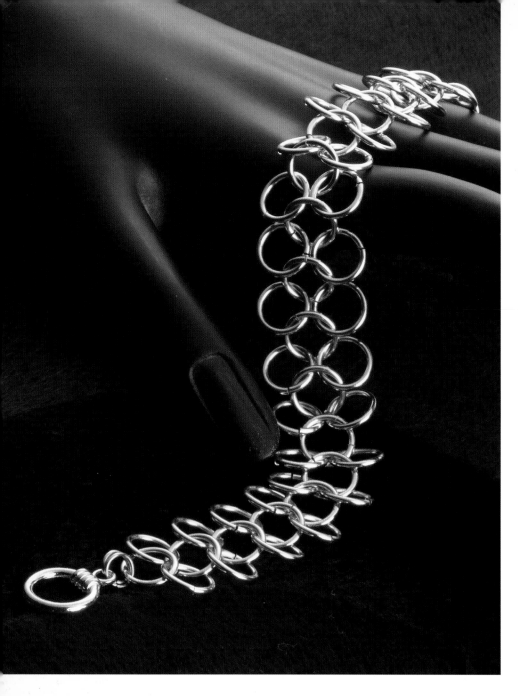

European "4 in 1" Bracelet

This bracelet employs a weave pattern common in European chain mail. Alternating rows and columns of this style are commonly thought to have been invented by the Celts many centuries ago.

SIZE: 8" including clasp

MATERIALS:
52 - 10mm Gold jump rings
4 - 6mm Gold jump rings (open)
Toggle clasp

INSTRUCTIONS:

Open 18 – 10mm jump rings; close 34 jump rings. Add 2 closed 10mm rings to an open ring. Close ring and lay open rings as shown in the diagram. You may want to pin the bracelet down to a board or tape to surface to hold work. With an open jump ring, pick up the two side rings by the inside edges, add two closed rings and close ring. Open out two rings again. Continue in this manner until bracelet is about 6" long. Add one more ring picking up side rings but without adding rings. To these single rings on each end of bracelet, add a 6mm jump ring and half of clasp. Add another 6mm jump ring beside this one through the clasp loop.

Beaded Lace "4 in 1" Bracelet

Topaz beads complement the beautiful gold rings in this Beaded Lace Bracelet. The bracelet also looks beautiful with Turquoise beads and silver rings.

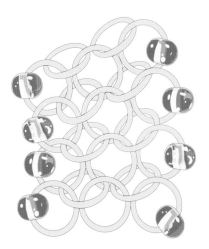

Thread E beads onto the outside jump rings.

SIZE: 7½" including clasp

MATERIALS:
117 - 8mm Gold jump rings
46 – Topaz E-beads
2 Lobster clasps ⅜"

INSTRUCTIONS:

Bracelet: Close 48 jump rings; open the remainder. Add 4 closed rings to an open ring. Close ring and lay open rings as shown. See Diagram. • With an open jump ring, pick up the last 2 rings going down into 1 and up in the second, add 2 closed rings and close ring. Open out 2 added rings. Continue in this manner until bracelet is about 7" long.

Beaded Edge: String an E-bead on an open jump ring and attach to 2 adjacent side rings, starting at one end of the bracelet. Add ring by going from a side ring that lies over the adjacent ring down into the next one. You will see a natural overlap along the side of the bracelet; if you don't see it, push the rings closer together. Close ring. • Open a second ring, add an E-bead, and go down in the last ring and down in the next ring along side. Continue along that side in the same manner. • Repeat for the other side of the bracelet, starting at the same end, or turn the bracelet over and work from the opposite end.

Clasp: Open unbeaded ending jump rings on one end and add 2 lobster clasps. Beads in edge rings may slide around into the bracelet but are easily rotated back in place.

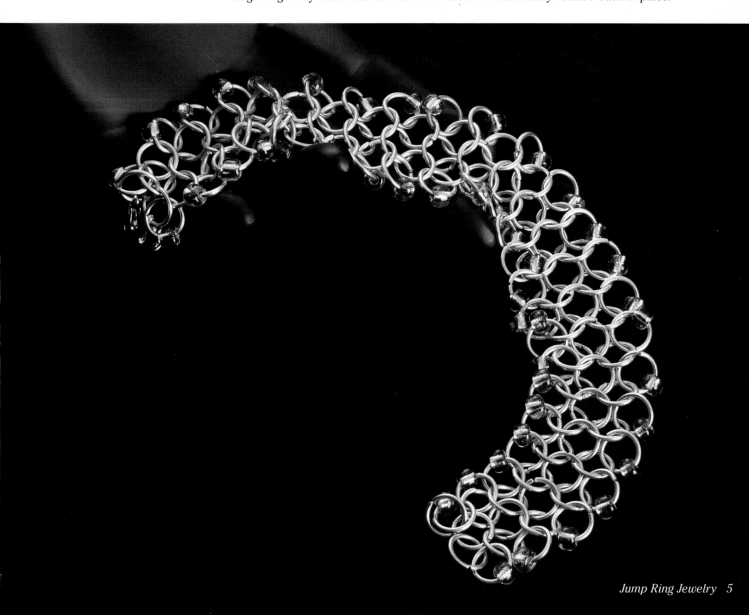

Begin with center strand.

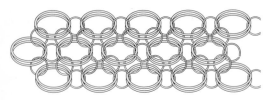

Add side strands.

Japanese Bracelet

Kusari, or Japanese chain mail came into use in the 14th century. Unlike the rows and columns of European mail, Japanese patterns tend to be very geometric, making the patterns ideal for beautiful, intricate-looking jewelry.

SIZE: 8"

MATERIALS:
92 - 9mm Gold jump rings
103 - 6mm Silver jump rings
S connector

INSTRUCTIONS:

Center Strand: Close all 9mm rings; open all 6mm rings. Slide 4 – 9mm jump rings on a 6mm ring and close ring. Pick up 2 of these 9mm rings with a 6mm ring and close. Continue chain until there are 16 sets of doubled 9mm rings long.

Side Strands: Make 2 more chains with 15 sets of doubled 9mm jump rings.

Assembly: Lay chains side by side with 16 set chain in the center. Outer doubled rings will lie next to 6mm links on the center chain. Connect chains with 6mm rings connecting outer doubled rings to 2 adjacent double rings in center chain. On one end, attach "S" connector to double jump rings. Close "S" connector by squeezing it with pliers. To wear, connect the other side of the "S" connector to doubled jump rings on the other end.

Jump Ring Earrings

A perfect match for the Jump Ring necklace, these earrings are also elegant when worn on their own.

SIZE: 1½"

MATERIALS:
8 – 9mm Silver jump rings
12 – 6mm Gold jump rings
8 – 5mm Copper jump rings
2 ear wires

INSTRUCTIONS:

Make a 4 set chain following Fringe instructions from Jump Ring necklace. Attach Silver and Copper jump rings through loop in ear wire.

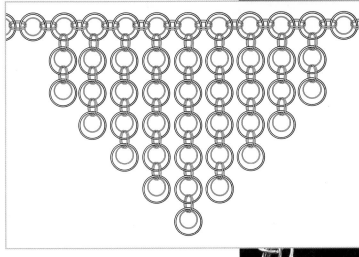

Jump Ring Necklace

Unique chic! Silver, gold and copper blend sumptuously in an attractive designer ensemble that you will be proud to claim as your own.

SIZE: 15"

MATERIALS:
77 - 9mm Silver jump rings
160 - 6mm Gold jump rings
77 - 5mm Copper jump rings
Toggle clasp

INSTRUCTIONS:

Necklace Base: Close all Silver jump rings and all Copper jump rings. Open all Gold jump rings. Pick up a Silver and a Copper ring on a Gold ring and close. Attach another Gold jump ring beside first. With another Gold jump ring, pick up one Silver and one Copper ring from first assembly and add a Silver ring and a Copper ring. Close Gold ring. Add another Gold ring beside this one.

• Repeat to continue chain until chain is about 14" long or 43 sets of Silver and Copper rings. End with Gold jump rings. On each end of chain, add 2 Gold jump rings and clasp. If you need to lengthen the necklace, add more sets of Silver and Copper rings in multiples of 2, so that strand will have an uneven number of sets.

Fringe: Make 2 chains each of 2, 3, 4 and 5 sets. Make 1 chain of 6 sets. Attach the 6 set chain to the center of the necklace with two Gold jump rings. Attach the 5 set strands on either side. Attach the 4 set chains on either side of the 5 set chains. Attach the 3 strand sets on either side of the 4 set chains. Attach the 2 set chains on either side of these.

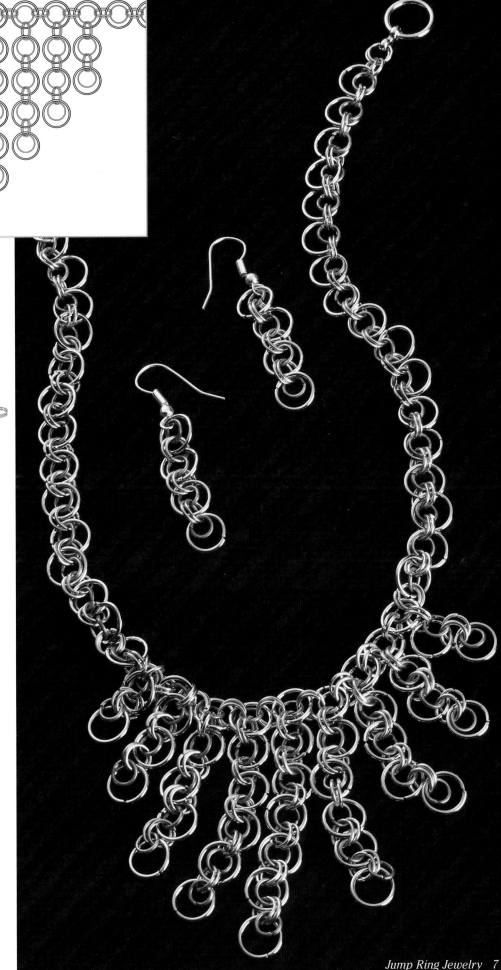

Turquoise and Silver Links Necklace

An exquisite example of the beauty that results when turquoise and silver are artfully paired, this Links necklace features a gorgeous turquoise donut medallion. Fringe dangles end in turquoise chips for a stunning finish.

SIZE: 24" plus 2½" fringe

MATERIALS:
Turquoise donut
6 Turquoise chips
38 - 6mm Silver jump rings
20 – 10mm Silver links with 2 loops
2 – 18" Gunmetal Black chains
Silver chain, fine cable
Silver toggle clasp

INSTRUCTIONS:
Necklace: Remove clasp and jump rings from black chain. Cut 8 – 2" lengths of Black chain and 4 – 2" lengths of Silver chain. Open all jump rings. Slide one end of a piece of Black chain, one end of a piece of Silver chain and one piece of Black chain onto a jump ring. Close jump ring. Attach a second jump ring to the other ends of the chain, sliding on chains in the same order and keeping them straight. Repeat to make 4 of these chain assemblies.
Slide 1 chain assembly through center of donut. Open a jump ring and slide on both jump rings of chain assembly, making sure the chains are not twisted. Slide on 1 link and close ring. Attach 2 more links with jump rings. Open a jump ring and attach a chain assembly. Open and attach a jump ring and a link. Continue to add links and jump rings until there are 7 on that side. Attach a jump ring and half of toggle clasp. Repeat for other side.

Fringe: Cut 2 – 8½" pieces of Black chain and 1 of Silver chain. Fold in half and put loop through hole in donut front to back. Bring ends through loop to form a Lark's Head knot. Pull down on ends to tighten fringe. Slide chips on jump rings and attach to ends of fringe chains. Chips may need to have holes enlarged to fit on jump rings. Choose small, flat chips for best results. If necessary, use a bead reamer or small drill bit and carefully enlarge holes. Substitute Silver spacers for chips if desired.

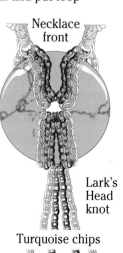

Necklace front

Lark's Head knot

Turquoise chips

Tube Bead Earrings

Earrings are a lovely gift, especially when they shimmer in your favorite color. Make a set for all your friends with this quick and easy technique.

SIZE: 1"

MATERIALS:
6 – 9mm jump rings
8 Lt. Blue faceted donut tube beads
Gold ear wires

INSTRUCTIONS:
Open a jump ring, slide on a tube bead and attach ring to ear wire. Close jump ring. Open second jump ring, slide through last tube bead, add another tube bead and close ring. Open a jump ring, slide through last tube bead, slide on 2 tube beads and close ring. Repeat for second earring. If longer earrings are desired, repeat second step until length desired.

Blue Tube Bead Necklace

Faceted beads radiate with their own sparkle and shine. Change the color of the bead and make jewelry to coordinate with everything in your wardrobe.

SIZE: 18"

MATERIALS:
55 - 9mm Gold jump rings
107 Lt. Blue Czech fire polished faceted donut tubes
Gold toggle clasp

Tip: This style of bead is found under a variety of names, including donut, barrel or tube beads. These tube beads are about 4mm long and 6mm in diameter. Each bead has a large hole that allows 2 jump rings to slide through it, but all jump rings and beads vary. Check your jump rings to make sure the wires slide through easily and don't lock up and break the bead when moved.

Tip: For a cleaner look to this piece, hide the jump ring slits inside the tube beads.

INSTRUCTIONS:
Open all jump rings. On a jump ring, slide on half the toggle clasp and a tube bead. Close jump ring. Take a second jump ring and slide through first tube bead. Slide on 2 tube beads and close jump ring. On a third jump ring, slide through a tube bead on last jump ring, placing second tube bead to one side of jump ring. On next jump ring, repeat process, placing the tube bead on the opposite side of the jump ring. Repeat this pattern 51 more times, alternating the non-connecting tube beads. Or, repeat until necklace is desired length. Open a jump ring and slide through last tube bead and the other half of the clasp. Close the jump ring.

Continue adding and alternating beads on jump rings.

Necklace toggle clasp

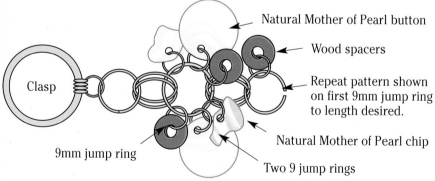

Natural Mother of Pearl button

Wood spacers

Repeat pattern shown
on first 9mm jump ring
to length desired.

Natural Mother of Pearl chip

Clasp

9mm jump ring

Two 9 jump rings

Shell Bangle Bracelet

Fabulous texture makes the Shell Bangle bracelet a joy to wear. The natural colors and pearlescent discs complement your entire wardrobe.

SIZE: 8" including clasp

MATERIALS:
40 - 9mm Gold jump rings
72 - 6mm Gold jump rings
Gold toggle clasp
24 Natural Mother of pearl buttons
24 Natural Mother of pearl chips
24 - 2mm x 7.5mm wood spacers

INSTRUCTIONS:

Bracelet Base: Open 14 - 9mm jump rings; close the rest. Make base bracelet from 9mm Gold jump rings by connecting 1 open jump ring, half of clasp and two closed jump rings. Attach an open jump ring to 2 closed rings and close. Continue in pattern and end with single jump ring and the other half of clasp. If you need a longer bracelet, add another double and single jump ring set, or add singles to both ends.

Bangles: Open 72 - 6mm jump rings. Divide jump rings into groups of 24. For the first group, slide a mother of pearl button onto each ring. Slide mother of pearl chips onto each ring of the second group, and a wood spacer on each ring in the last group. Connect 2 of each to the single 9mm jump rings on the base bracelet, one on each side. Since chips are different sizes, some may not string onto a jump ring. Choose chips that are thinner and have a hole close to the edge.

Rope Links and Chain

Brighten your day with this glittering ensemble. Tantalizing bright gold sparkles in the sunlight, inviting everyone to take a closer look.

This beautiful necklace can be worn all one length or wrapped around twice.

SIZE:
64" necklace, 2" earrings

MATERIALS:
10 - 25mm Gold rope circles
18 - 15mm Gold rope squares
36 - 10mm Gold jump rings
3 - 18" Gold chains
2 Gold ear wires

INSTRUCTIONS:

Necklace: Remove clasps and jump rings from chains. Cut chain into 5" lengths. To one end of a chain length, attach a jump ring and rope square. Close jump ring. Attach another jump ring to rope square and add a rope circle. Close jump ring. Attach another jump ring and add a rope square. Add a jump ring and attach a chain length. Repeat pattern ending with a jump ring and attach to first chain.

Earrings: Attach jump ring to rope square and ear wire. Attach jump ring to square and add a rope circle. Close jump ring. Repeat for second earring.

Pendant Side View

Cut chain links and drop through the hole in a pendant. Open a 6mm jump ring and attach to both ends of a chain.

Attach 2 leaves to one jump ring and 1 leaf to the other jump ring.

Glass Pendant with Gold Leaves

Simply elegant, the Green Glass Pendant shimmers from a classic bright gold chain. Dangling gold leaves add an eye-catching finish.

SIZE: 20" plus 2" pendant

MATERIALS:
⅞" x 1¼" Green glass pendant with hole from front to back
24" carved Gold cable chain
11 - 10mm Gold jump rings
3 - 6mm Gold jump rings
3 Gold spacer leaves

INSTRUCTIONS:
Prep: Open all jump rings. Remove clasp and jump rings from chain. Cut 6 – 11 link pieces of chain and 4 – 19 link pieces of chain.

Pendant: Cut a length of 14 chain links and drop through hole in pendant. Open a 6mm jump ring and attach to both ends of chain.

Necklace: Open a 10mm jump ring and slide on 6mm jump ring and 2 pieces of chain 11 links long. Close jump rings. • Open 2 - 10mm jump rings and attach to ends of chain. Slide on a 19 link piece of chain on each and close. Repeat procedure alternating 11 and 19 link pieces of chain. End with jump rings. On one side, attach lobster clasp to last jump ring.

Finish: Open 2 – 6mm jump rings. On one, slide on 2 leaves; on the other, slide on 1 leaf. Link together and attach single leaf jump ring to pendant chain so that it falls against pendant.

Adding Beads
Drop a ⅝" chain through a bead then secure it with a second jump ring.

Attaching the Clasp
Attach jump rings to end of chains and add clasp on the ends for closure.

Two-Strand Necklace with Wooden Beads

Dainty wood beads float on delicate chains of bright gold in an elegant necklace that will complement your wardrobe beautifully.

SIZE: 24"

MATERIALS:
14 - 9mm printed wood barrel beads
44" Gold chain, fine cable
32 - Gold 6mm jump rings
Gold toggle clasp

INSTRUCTIONS:
Cut 14 - 2" lengths of chain, 2 – 1" lengths and 14 - ⅝" lengths of chain.
• Open all jump rings. On a jump ring, slide on a 2" chain and a ⅝" chain and close the ring. Drop the ⅝" chain through a bead and hold bead and jump ring while catching the other end of the chain with a jump ring. Slide on a 2" chain and close ring. On the 2" end, add a jump ring and a ⅝" chain and close. Repeat steps to create a necklace of 8 - 2" chain lengths. End with a 2" length.
• On each end, add a jump ring and half a clasp. Make another similar chain beginning with a 1" chain length, 6 – 2" chain lengths and a 1" chain length on the end. Attach jump rings on both ends and attach to the clasp.

Silver and Gold Necklace with Gold Leaves

You are about to become more beautiful! The classic interlock design encircles your neck in sumptuous silver and gold that flatters any skin tone.

SIZE: 15"

MATERIALS:
51 - 9mm Gold jump rings,
95 - 6mm Silver jump rings
9 Gold leaf spacers, leaves drilled side-to-side.
Silver or Gold lobster clasp

INSTRUCTIONS:
Close all Gold jump rings; open all Silver jump rings. Attach a Silver ring to 2 Gold rings and close ring. Attach a Silver ring to one end of chain and attach another Gold ring; close ring. Continue to create chain until it is at least 14" long (33 Gold, 32 Silver jump rings).
Attach a Silver jump ring to each leaf and close the rings.
Lay chain out so that all Gold rings are flat and are lying in the same direction. Silver rings will be at right angles and standing up. Begin in center set of three Gold rings and attach two Gold rings with Silver rings to outside two rings. Close rings. Attach two Silver rings from these two rings to center ring of set of three. Attach a Silver ring to bottom of set of two rings and pick up one leaf assembly. Attach a second Silver ring to the other Gold bottom ring and through ring in leaf. Make four more of these on each side of center.
TIP: This necklace sits at the base of the neck. If desired, add Silver and Gold jump rings to necklace to make it longer (evenly on each side). On the last Gold jump ring, attach a lobster clasp.

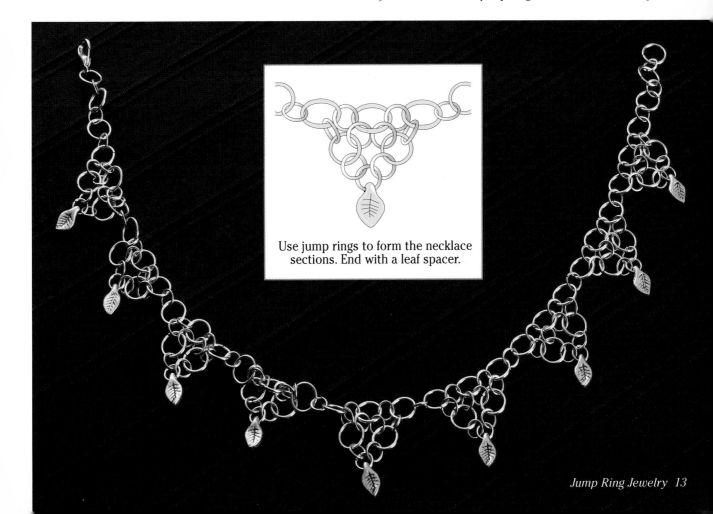

Use jump rings to form the necklace sections. End with a leaf spacer.

Mother of Pearl Bracelet

Elegant opalescent pearl disks encompass your wrist with graceful radiance.

SIZE: 9"

MATERIALS:
16 Mother of Pearl 4-Hole Rounds
98 - 8mm Gold jump rings
Gold toggle clasp

INSTRUCTIONS:

Close 24 jump rings and open the remainder. Attach 1 Mother of Pearl round to 2 rounds by adjacent holes. On 1 side, attach 1 more round. Continue this pattern, a row of 1, then a row of 2, using all rounds. End with a row of 1.

• On sides, in between rounds, open a jump ring, attach to one round. Add 2 closed jump rings and close ring. Open another ring, slide in hole in next round and pick up closed jump rings. Close ring. Do this in all outside adjacent holes, including the ends.

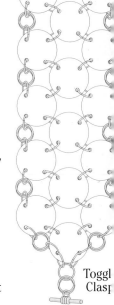

Toggle Clasp

Clasp: Attach 1 jump ring in each end hole. Close rings. Open a jump ring and pick up both of these rings. Close ring. Open 2 rings and attach side by side to last closed ring and clasp. Close rings. Repeat for other end of bracelet with second half of clasp. To shorten this bracelet, leave off last 3 rounds. This makes a 7½" bracelet. You can also use smaller jump rings in the clasp attachment section.

Double Chain Bracelet

Pretty for both every-day and evening wear, the Double Chain bracelet wraps your wrist in beautiful shiny silver.

SIZE: 8" including clasp

MATERIALS:
100 - 6mm metal ring beads
104 - 6mm Silver jump rings
Silver metal toggle clasp,
    oval and double links

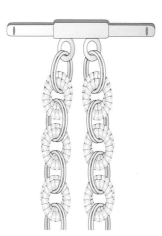

Tip: For this bracelet, 2 Chain-nose pliers or a Chain-nose and a Bent-nose pliers are recommended as the spacing is tight.

INSTRUCTIONS:

Open all jump rings. On a jump ring, slide on 4 metal ring beads. Close ring. Add another jump ring next to first and close. Pick up 2 metal ring beads with a jump ring and add 2 ring beads. Close jump ring. Add another jump ring next to it. Continue chain until it is 7½" long. End with 2 jump rings. Make another chain the same length. Attach chains to double clasp with ending jump rings.

Clasp

"Y" Necklace with Earrings

Blue clusters burst into flower along a golden chain. Perfect with your favorite white silk blouse or T-shirt and jeans, this addition to your accessory wardrobe is so pretty, you will want to wear it all the time.

SIZE: Necklace: 16" plus 1½" dangle, Earrings: 1½"

MATERIALS:
1 – 24" carved Gold cable chain
16 - 9mm Gold jump rings
108 - 6mm Gold jump rings
108 Blue E beads
Gold toggle clasp
2 Gold ear wires

INSTRUCTIONS:

Earrings: Remove clasp and small jump rings from chain. Cut 2 pieces of chain 9 links long. Attach one end to ear wire. Attach the other end to a 9mm jump ring. Open 12 – 6mm jump rings and string an E bead on each, using 4 of each of 3 bead colors in mix. Attach these jump rings to 9mm jump ring. Repeat for second earring.

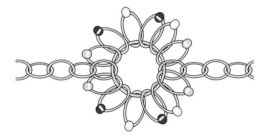

Necklace: Cut 13 pieces of chain 9 links long. If you desire to make the chain segments longer, use an uneven number of links to allow the components to fall in the right direction.

Connect 3 chain segments to a 9mm jump ring and close ring. Attach a 9mm jump ring to each end. Arrange segments in a Y. Attach remaining chain segments with 9mm jump rings evenly on both sides. End with a jump ring and attach clasp on each side before closing ring.

Make 84 beaded jump rings as for earrings. Attach 12 – 6mm beaded jump rings to 3 jump rings above junction on each side, attaching 6 on each side of jump ring. Attach 12 – 6mm beaded jump rings to ending jump ring.

Big Jump Rings Byzantine Chain Bracelet

by Donna Thomason

Perfectly elegant, this shining bracelet with mega size jump rings is easy to make. It brings attention wherever you go. The beautiful design is one of the first European links to be developed... the Byzantine Chain is also known as the Bird's Nest.

SIZE: 8½" including clasp

MATERIALS:

4 feet of Sterling Silver 16 gauge wire
1 Silver toggle clasp
³⁄₁₆" wood dowel or *Beadalon* Jump Ring Maker tool 6mm mandrel
4" of string or thin wire

INSTRUCTIONS:

Make Jump Rings: Wrap wire around a metal mandrel or wood dowel. Slip the coil off of the mandrel (page 3). Cut jump rings apart with wire cutters or a jeweler's saw. Make 122 jump rings.

Bracelet: Open 120 jump rings. • 1. Close 2 jump rings. Tie a string or wire around the 2 rings to make the links easy to grasp. • 2. Add a pair of rings to the starting pair. Close both rings. Link a second pair to make a set of 3. • 3. Separate the third pair and let them flop down, 1 on each side. • 4. Separate the second pair (in the center). • 5. Link another pair through the exposed loops (in the center). • Repeat until the bracelet is 8" long.

Clasp: Remove the string or wire. Add a clasp section to each end of the bracelet with 1 jump ring.

Separate center rings ➘

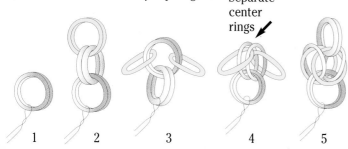

1   2   3   4   5

INSTRUCTIONS:

Center Chains: Cut a 2" piece of fine cable chain and a 3" piece of medium wide cable chain. For side chains, cut 2 – 1" pieces of fine cable chain and 2 – 2½" medium wide cable chain. Attach 4mm jump rings to each end of chain pieces. Slide chains onto necklace through jump rings.

Assembly: Unscrew ball from necklace. Slide on 1 Silver melon bead, 4 jet barrel beads, 1 melon bead, 4 barrel beads, 1 melon bead, medium cable chain, 1 melon bead, fine cable chain, and 3 barrel beads. • Carefully slide beads to end of necklace and attach the other end of the fine cable chain, 1 melon bead and the other end of the medium cable chain. Slide on 1 melon bead, two barrel beads, 1 melon bead, center medium chain, melon bead, center fine chain and 5 barrel beads. • Slide center beads to end of necklace and attach second jump ring of fine chain, a melon bead and second jump ring of medium chain. Slide on a melon bead, 2 barrel beads, a melon bead, a side medium chain, melon bead, side fine chain, and 3 barrel beads. • Slide side assembly to end of necklace and attach second jump ring of fine chain, melon bead, second jump ring of medium chain and melon bead. Slide on 4 barrel beads, a melon bead, 4 barrel beads and a melon bead. Screw on ball of necklace.

Ðoop Earrings

Top off your evening with gorgeous silver and black earrings.

SIZE: 2"

MATERIALS:
Fine cable chain, 2 - 1" lengths
Medium wide cable chain, 2 - 2" lengths
8 – 4mm Silver jump rings
6 Silver melon beads
12 jet barrel beads
1" Silver beading hoops
Earring wires

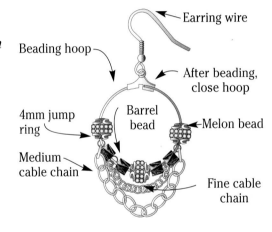

INSTRUCTIONS:

Attach 4mm jump rings to ends of chains. Open hoop. String a melon bead, medium cable chain, barrel bead, fine cable chain, barrel bead, melon bead, barrel bead, fine chain, barrel bead, medium chain and a melon bead. Close hoop. Open earring wire loop and attach to hoop. Close the loop.

Ðoop Necklace

Absolutely elegant, this sparkling evening accessory will dazzle everyone at your next dinner party.

Combine an assortment of jet black and silver beads to create a stunning necklace that dangles as shimmers everywhere you go.

SIZE: 17"

MATERIALS:
5" Fine cable chain
8" Medium wide cable chain
12 - 4mm Silver jump rings
16 - 8 x 8.5mm Silver metal
     melon beads
31 - 6mm jet barrel beads
Silver ball hoop necklace

Hoop Necklace

Rainbow Bracelet

What fun! Brighten your day with a rainbow of color. This casual bracelet will win compliments from your friends.

SIZE: 8" including clasp

MATERIALS:
6" Silver fine cable chain
12 glass bead roundels (Large holes)
15 - 6mm Silver jump rings
Silver lobster clasp

INSTRUCTIONS:
Cut 12 - ⅜" pieces of chain. Open all jump rings. Arrange roundels in rainbow pattern as shown or as desired. Attach a jump ring to one end of a chain length and thread on first roundel bead. Attach jump ring to end of chain, add another chain to jump ring and close ring. Continue using all roundels and end with a jump ring. Open jump ring at beginning of bracelet and attach lobster clasp. Close jump ring. Attach a jump ring to the other end and close.

Hearts & Flowers Charm Bracelet

Delightfully charming! If you love charm bracelets, this must-have accessory will steal your heart.

SIZE: 8" including clasp

MATERIALS:
53 - 9mm Silver jump rings
12 – 6mm Silver jump rings
12 Heart charms
Silver toggle clasp

INSTRUCTIONS:
Flower: Close one 9mm jump ring and open two 9mm jump rings. Slide one jump ring through closed ring and close. Stack these 2 jump rings and slide third jump ring through both rings. Close jump ring. This is one flower.
• Make 13 flowers for an 8" bracelet.

Assembly: Open a 9mm jump ring and slide on a flower and half of clasp. (Make sure you keep the flower rings stacked together so there is one single center hole.) Close ring. • Open another 9mm jump ring and slide on first flower and another flower; close ring. Continue in this pattern ending with a single jump ring and other half of clasp.

Charms: Open 12 – 6mm jump rings and slide on charms. Lay out bracelet and place charms along bracelet, alternating sides. The ending 9mm jump rings will not have charms. When you like the arrangement of the charms, attach the 6mm jump rings to the single 9mm rings; close rings.